What Do They Say about Tay?

The release of "Tay and Friends: Tay Learns to Code" is a fantastic addition to early science readers. This engaging book not only introduces young readers to the world of coding but also teaches them valuable problem-solving skills. The story emphasizes the idea that robots are great problem solvers but may require new codes to overcome challenges, instilling a sense of creativity and adaptability in young minds. The colorful illustrations and relatable characters make learning about coding an enjoyable adventure. This book is a must-have for parents and teachers looking to introduce coding concepts to children in a fun and accessible way. It's a delightful journey into the world of technology and problem-solving that will leave kids excited about the possibilities of coding.
- Catherine Togba, founder of *Black Parent Magazine*

This book is dedicated to all my students who color outside of the lines. This is where creativity is found.

♥ PEL

Me on the Page Publishing
Copyright © 2024 Phelicia Lang M.Ed.

ISBN-13: 979-8-9855827-6-5

This book is sold subject to the condition that it shall not, by way of trade or otherwise, be lent, resold, hired out or otherwise circulated without the publisher's prior consent in any form of binding or cover other than that in which it is published and without a similar condition including
this condition being imposed on the subsequent publisher.
The moral right of the author has been asserted.

Illustrations Copyright © Phelicia Lang M.Ed.

Illustrations by Vicky Amrullah (Uzuri Designs)

TAY AND FRIENDS

Tay Learns to Code

Book 2

Dear Family,

Our world is filled with many fun things to explore, and your child is filled with wonder and amazement of how things work! Cultivate their interest by reading great books and providing opportunities for them to think like a Scientist, Technologist, Engineer or Mathematician.

This book will have challenging words as your child moves from **learning to read**, to **reading to learn**. Little scientists will need to use non-fiction text skills to navigate the pages.

You can help them by using the strategy support graphics on the next few pages.

I'm sure you will say :"Hey, that's Me on the Page!"
as they make connections while reading
Tay and Friends: Tay Learns to Code!

Stay safe and Be Well,

Phelicia Lang

Learning to Read Strategies (K-2)

Look at the whole word 👀	math
Put your finger under the beginning letter of the word.	math 👆
Look for letter teams and patterns you might know.	m a(th)
Slide your finger from left to right slowly stretching out the letter sounds and teams in the word.	m a(th) ··· →
Blend the sounds together to read the word.	m a(th) →

As they **Read to Learn** (2-5), think...

- Does my word make sense?
- Does my word look right?
- Does my word sound right?

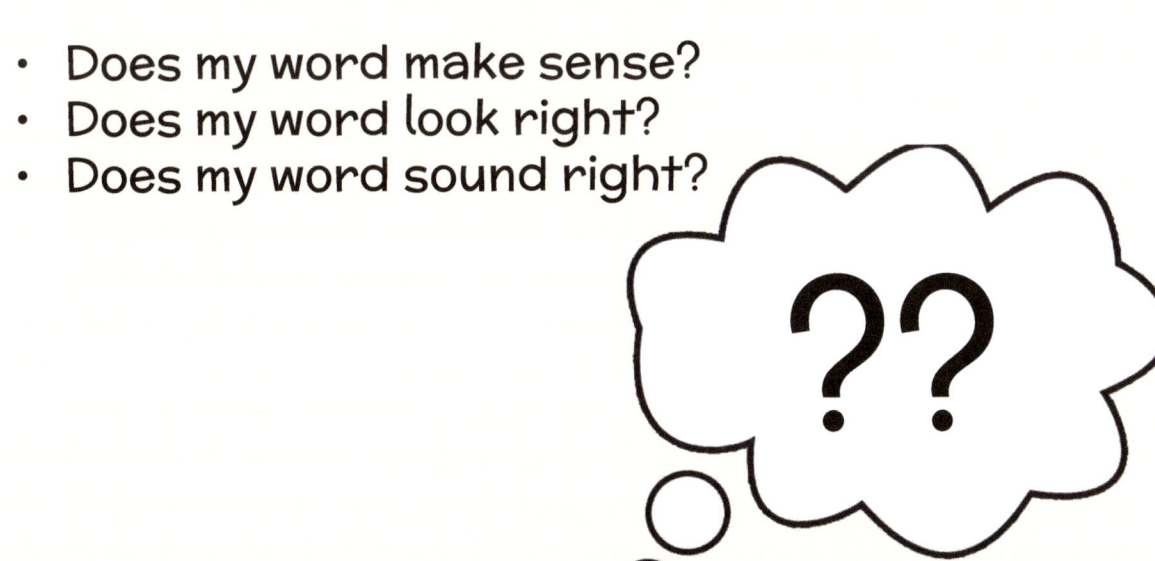

Non-fiction Text Features in this Book

## Label A word next to a picture that identifies what it is.	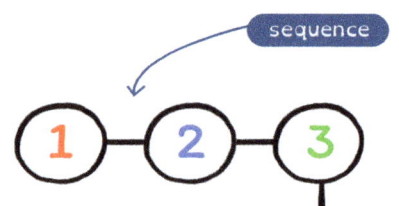
## Keyword Important vocabulary words in the text that may be bold, italics, or colored.	ving it direction ed **coding**.
## Glossary A page near the back of the book where you can find the meanings of the keywords.	 Sequence: one thing following another Code: a set of direct by a computer

Captions

A title or words underneath a picture that tells about the picture above it.

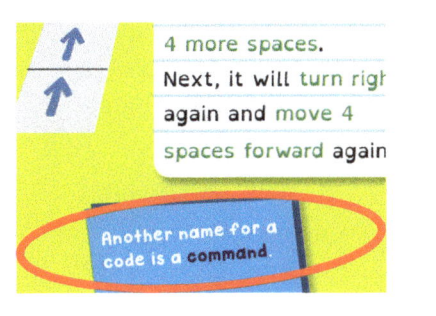

Tay Learns to Code

This is Tay.

He is smart
and very kind.

He loves to figure
out how things work.

Tay loves to
make new things.

Tay and his dad have made lots of robots.

Now he will learn how to make a robot move.

Making the robot move and giving it directions, is called **coding**.

Coding is used in computers, and video games to make things move.

First, Tay will draw a map of where he wants the robot to move.

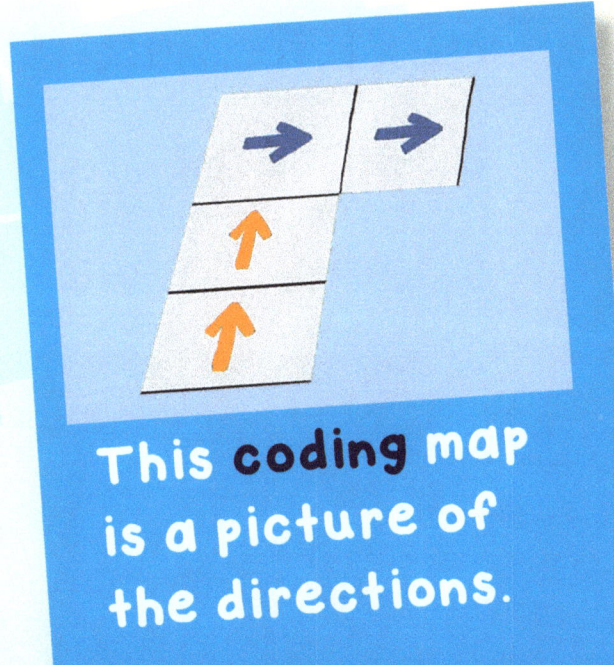

This **coding map** is a picture of the directions.

Next, he **commands** the robot to go straight 4 spaces.

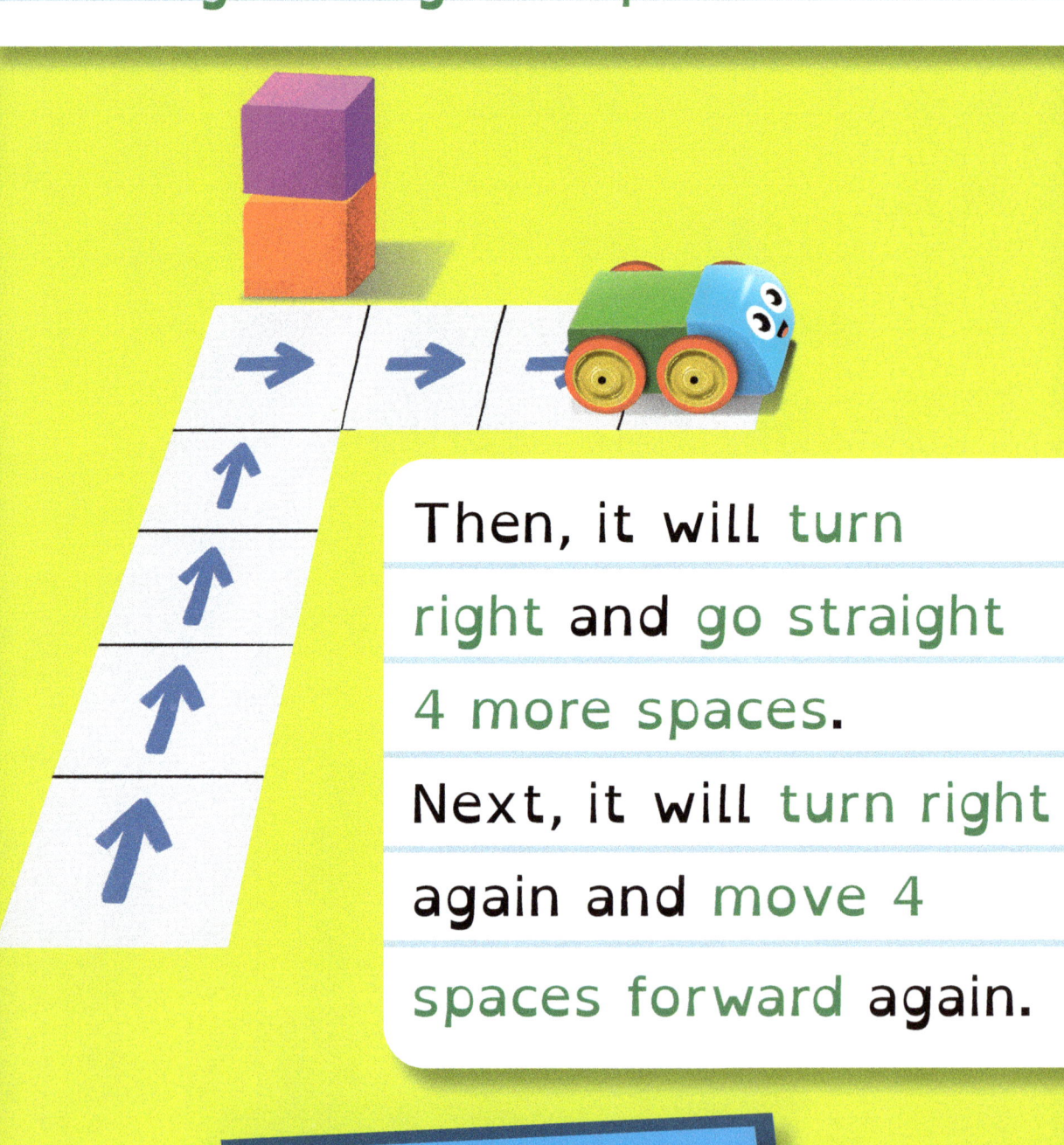

Then, it will turn right and go straight 4 more spaces. Next, it will turn right again and move 4 spaces forward again.

Another name for a code is a **command**.

Finally, it will take another right turn and go straight 4 spaces.

The robot is back where it started!

They see that it is very important to give the robot directions in order.

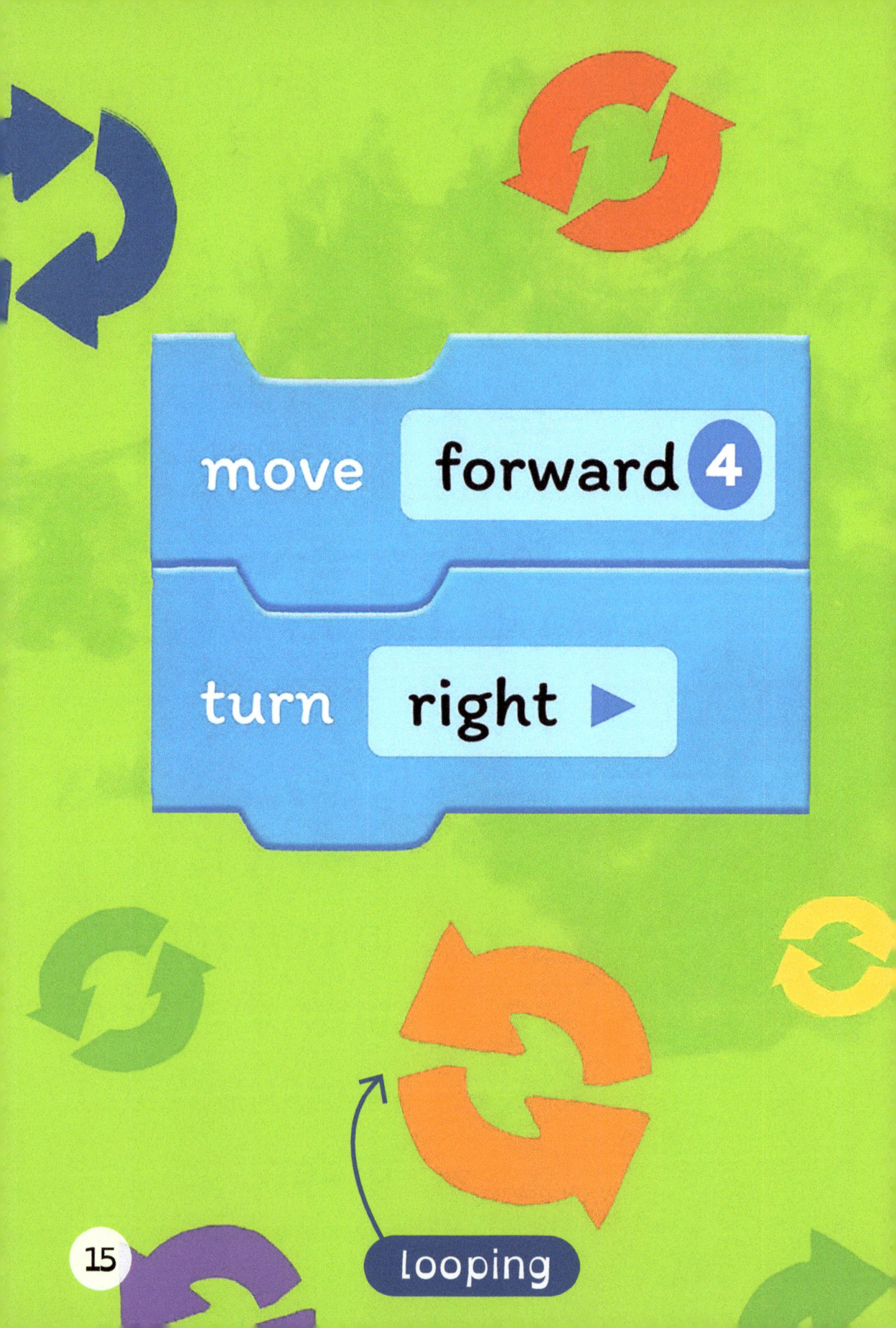

parenthesis

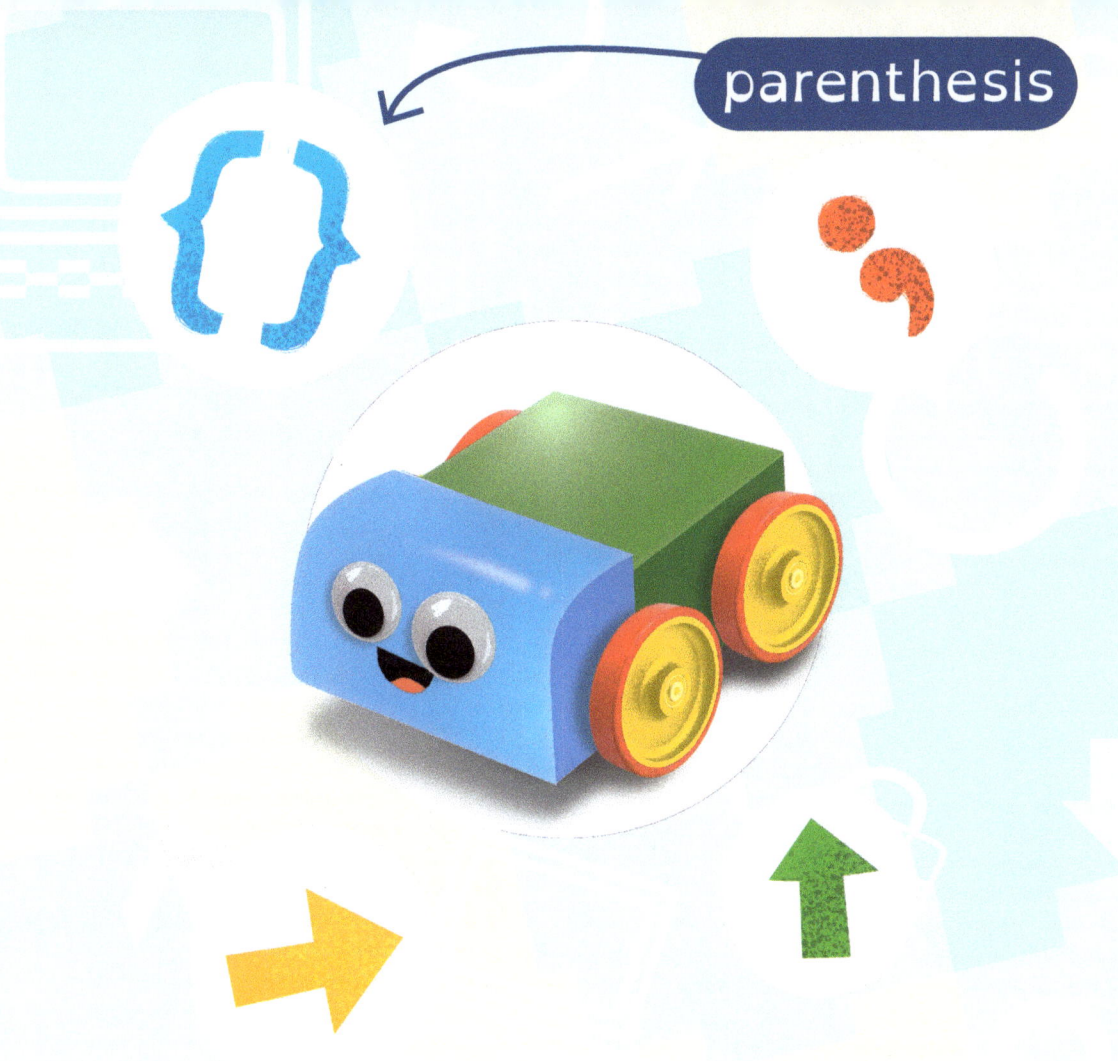

Aleeyah and Raj think the robot can follow the same commands again, and again. This is called **looping**.

Tay and his friends begin to give the robot **commands** on an obstacle course built by his Grandpa.

The robot goes straight and stops at a curve. Why did this happen? This is a **problem**.

Tay and his friends take turns to **solve** the **problem**.

Raj thinks the robot knows how to move in a straight line but does not know what to do when it comes to a curve.

They must work together to **solve** this **problem**, just like real scientists.

Robots are good at following directions in order or a **sequence**. The friends need to tell the robot what to do if it comes to a curve. They will need to make a new map and **code**.

Tay and his dad have never done this before so they call an expert: cousin Kimber!

Kimber has learned a lot about computer engineering and robots in college.

Amber Green graduated from The Ohio State University with a degree in electrical engineering. She is currently a PhD student at the University of Michigan studying robotics. Amber loves learning about how robots can make our lives easier.

Hi Cousin Kimber! Dad helped us build a robot and we don't know how to help it make turns.

Hey there engineer! It sounds like you need an **if-then-statement**. In **coding**, **if-then statements** are called conditional statements.

If-then statements are like rules that the computer uses to make decisions.

We make decisions too:

If {raining at school} = true

Then {students stay inside}

Else {students go outside to play}

OH! I get it!! If, the robot comes to a left curve is true, then it leans left on the path.

Yes! The code is written like this:
If {robot comes to a left curve=true} **then**{lean left on the path} **else** {keep following the path}.

If the robot comes to a right curve is true, then it leans right on the path.

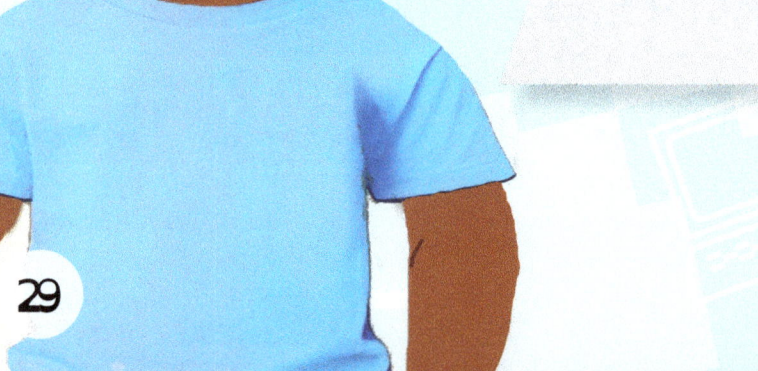

IF {robot comes to a right curve=true **then** {lean right on the path} **else** {keep following the path.

Their plan worked, and the **problem** is solved! They all cheer!

It's time for his friends to go home. They all had fun with the robot.

Just like Tay and Friends, you can dream big dreams and be kind too!

What will you be?

Dear Young Scientist,

In *Tay Learns to Code*, you learned what it means to code. You also learned how to use code to make a robot move.

Did you know that the science of writing codes and lanuages to give robots commands is called Computer programming? Yes, Programming!!

Just like Tay and Friends, you are on your way to learning more about STEM (Science, Technology, Engineering and Math).

You will do great things! Learning how things work and looking for answers to your questions is the secret to becoming a great scientist.

Stay curious and find the answers to your whys!

Phelicia Lang

Glossary

Sequence: one thing following another

Code: a set of directions used by a computer

Program: a series of directions for the computer to follow

Loop: a set of directions a computer will repeat

Problem: a challenge

If-then-else: a way to tell a computer what to do if a certain change/challenge appears

Symbols: pictures of commands

Scientist: a person who studies and researches a certain area of sciences to find answers and solutions

Solution: the answer to a problem

Command: directions given to a computer to tell it what to do the computer to follow

About the Author

Phelicia is a loving wife to Tony, and mother to four wonderful children, and precious grandchildren. They have all inspired her journey to find good books to reflect their lives and interests.

As a Reading Specialist, she's passionate about finding the right books to help readers connect to stories they love and books that reflect the readers.

Dreaming big dreams and using those dreams and gifts to help others, is the message she shares with her students.

When she's not creating on her computer she can be found Dreaming Big Dreams, reading and shopping.

More Books by Phelicia Lang

Tay Book Series

Mari Book Series

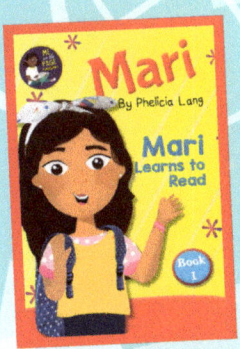

www.meonthepage.com

What did you think of *Tay Learns to Code*?

If you liked this book, I'd love to hear from you. I hope you can take a little time to review it on Amazon.

Find my books on Amazon

Reviews help me to write better books and they help others to choose great books.

If you're interested in coding, check out these websites and games:

Scratch Jr   scratchjr.org

Osmo Jr   playosmo.com

Botley   botleybot.com